A Gift for:

From:

Date:

A Good Day

A GIFT OF GRATITUDE

Brother David Steindl-Rast

In collaboration with Louie Schwartzberg

STERLING ETHOS
New York

STERLING ETHOS
New York

An Imprint of Sterling Publishing
387 Park Avenue South
New York, NY 10016

Text © 2013 by Brother David Steindl-Rast
Photographs by Louis Schwartzberg and Blacklight Films
Afterword by Louie Schwartzberg
For DVD copyright information and photo credits, see page 96

ISBN 978-1-4549-0798-5

Distributed in Canada by Sterling Publishing
c/o Canadian Manda Group, 165 Dufferin Street
Toronto, Ontario, Canada M6K 3H6
Distributed in the United Kingdom by GMC Distribution Services
Castle Place, 166 High Street, Lewes, East Sussex, England BN7 1XU
Distributed in Australia by Capricorn Link (Australia) Pty. Ltd.
P.O. Box 704, Windsor, NSW 2756, Australia

For information about custom editions, special sales, and premium and corporate purchases, please contact
Sterling Special Sales at 800-805-5489 or specialsales@sterlingpublishing.com.

Manufactured in China

2 4 6 8 10 9 7 5 3 1

www.sterlingpublishing.com

Contents

Dedicated to

"A NETWORK FOR GRATEFUL LIVING"

(Gratefulness.org)

∞

To my parents, Joseph and Eva, who were Holocaust survivors. They taught me to appreciate the little things in life, like food on the table, a roof over your head, and the blessings of having children. I am very grateful to the millions of viewers who shared the *Gratitude* video and made it a viral Internet sensation, which opened the door to this book being published.

— Louie Schwartzberg

Foreword

How a Brief Message Reached Millions

In 2006, friends of Benedictine monk, author, and lecturer Br. David Steindl-Rast invited him to record two short meditations about gratefulness, to be set to music by award-winning composer Gary Malkin. We simply intended to include these pieces in a promotional CD about the organization that Br. David co-founded, A Network for Grateful Living (ANG*L).

The meditations, spontaneously spoken, flowed from a heart honed by decades of prayer, practice, and sharing. Br. David offers this description of what happened: "It was early on a bright California morning. Gary invited me to sit down in front of the microphone and wish an imaginary audience a good day. After a moment's silence, I simply spoke from my heart. This was it. No re-takes. No additions. What you hear is that morning's message."

The meditations were given over to Gary, who scored chords, textures, and rhythms directly to the intimate tone of Br. David's voice, drawing forth all the soulfulness embedded in his words. We were quick to notice the inspirational potential of these montages. With the help of radio and television producer Jan St. John, who taped the original recordings in the studio of Chris and Barbara Wilson of Mill Valley, California, we started exploring their broader potential as YouTube videos that could be embedded on our website, www.gratefulness.org, which provides free interactive services for the practice of grateful living to people around the world. Chris served as executive producer, Jan as producer, and video editor Alejandro Torres matched the audio with photos selected with exquisite care by ANG*L's Community Development Coordinator Margaret Wakeley.

The results had that intangible extra ingredient—one that emerges when talented individuals work together towards a greater good. In June 2007, we gave birth to "A Good Day"; another video, "Giver of All Good Gifts," followed at Thanksgiving.

These videos, especially "A Good Day," rapidly garnered a strong following on the Internet. With very little promotion, within two weeks it had been viewed by four thousand people. Before long, requests started pouring in for DVDs and an MP4. Margaret had her hands full responding to emails we received, such as these:

"Please help. I am a Buddhist chaplain to four prisons in the U.K. The prisoners I see all lack gratitude, for obvious reasons. Some are very damaged. But I feel that this can be turned around by cultivating gratefulness. Where can I obtain a DVD copy of 'A GOOD DAY'?"

"I work for the Canadian Institute of Natural and Integrative Medicine, and we are launching an online program for people experiencing depression. One of the videos that was chosen to be used in the program is 'A Good Day with Brother David.' People found it inspiring and useful for those who are struggling."

"With all my heart, I thank you for the two DVDs of Brother David. I'm so delighted to have these films for use in the Living Spiritual Elders Project!"

"We will be using this video clip to help prepare our students for a silent 'meditation walk.'"

"I am a leader in a health care organization and I will be sharing this video at leadership, staff, and physician meetings for the next few months. My hope is that by encouraging openness, authenticity, and gratefulness, we will level the hierarchy that can sometimes get in the way of ensuring absolute safety for our patients and staff each and every time we provide care."

"This year we have adopted a new fund-raising model and did our first fund-raising event (a breakfast gathering) and had 150 people attend. We used 'A Good Day' for the benediction/invocation before breakfast and it was very well received. I am certain it is one of the reasons that our event was so successful!"

In 2010, Gary Malkin approached us to secure a release for Br. David's spoken word on the audio track. This release allowed Louie Schwartzberg, with whom Gary had been working, to proceed with a film that incorporated Br. David's voice and Gary's music as key soundtrack components. Soon people from all over the world started sending us a link to an eloquently moving TED lecture that contained gorgeous film footage by Louie overlaid with music by Gary Malkin and with Br. David's voice from a "A Good Day." Thus began further collaboration towards the creation of the book you now hold in your hands.

As of this writing, the sound track that Br. David and Gary created has, in various forms, been heard by some four million people around the world. Some people like it so much that they post their own set of pictures with it on YouTube. A psychiatrist prescribes "A Good Day" to his patients as daily reading. It has been used in churches, with chronic-pain patients, for organizational effectiveness groups, in a "compassionate care" section for young health professionals, to support ecological sustainability, by the Mind & Life Institute with His Holiness the Dalai Lama, with hospice volunteers, in courses on prayer, with grieving teenagers . . . the list goes on and on. Perhaps most profoundly of all, it is used by individuals on their own paths towards wholeness. Since it is for the healing of each of us and our earth that these words and their accompanying music came into being, it is fitting to let the voices of those influenced by them have the closing say:

"I woke this morning not even wanting to get out of bed because of the turmoil in my life at this time. My dearest lifelong friend has been diagnosed with the second melanoma, another close friend has a wife recently discovered to have cancer, and I'm fighting my own battle with greatly reduced mobility and several treatments a week for that. I came to the computer to see if anyone else had written a concerned note for my friend of all but four years of my life. What I found instead was astounding. The Gratefulness.org newsletter and the invitation to view a video about 'A Good Day' waited in the inbox. I hastily skimmed the email and went to Gratefulness and turned on the video. The words and pictures touched me in a way few things have. All I could think to do was quickly thank God for your ministry and then let the sights and healing words wash over me. I wept almost the whole way through it."

"I come to this site every morning, to center myself briefly and prepare for the day ahead. Recently your beautiful video has inspired me to add to my daily meditation practice: with each breath in I say silently 'thanks' and with each breath out, 'blessings.' Thank you for being here."

"Hardly a day goes by when I don't view this marvelous video by Brother David. It is not only inspirational and uplifting, but it is universal in its message. Let it speak to your inner being and deliver the message you may be seeking this very day."

— *Patricia Campbell Carlson*, Executive Director
A Network for Grateful Living
www.gratefulness.org
Ithaca, NY

"A Good Day" and
the Meaning of Gratefulness

"A Good Day" points to the gift of life and the only appropriate response to that gift: gratefulness. What do we really mean by gratefulness? As a basic definition, I would suggest that two things have to come into it. The first is appreciation. If you do not appreciate something, obviously you are not grateful for it. What does this appreciation mean? It is certainly different from having something appraised: Then you get the monetary value for it. Appreciation has very little to do with monetary value. If you walk on the beach and you pick up a beautiful shell, you really appreciate it, but its monetary value may be practically nothing. You appreciate it for its beautiful shape and color, for the occasion on which you found it, for the person you want to give it to . . . all sorts of things that have nothing to do with the monetary value.

In our society, we are inclined to think of how much something is worth monetarily. There is a completely different worth, and gratefulness points towards that worth that cannot be expressed in monetary terms, that cannot be quantified at all. It has nothing to do with quantity and everything to do with quality. Qualitatively you greatly appreciate it. It is valuable to you even if it has no monetary value at all.

You appreciate it also as *given*. It is so valuable, and yet it is given to you completely freely. These two things must come together. Maybe it's something simple—just that someone holds the door open for you, which means something to you and brings home the kindness that surrounds us, making it possible for us to be here. We should think how much work and kindness and engagement it takes for this planet to keep running. When I travel, I think of the hundreds of little bolts it took to put together the airplane that's carrying me. Somebody tightened each one of these bolts. That's a person I will never see in my life. I will never know the name of that person, but if even one or two of the most important bolts weren't secure, everyone who rides the airplane would be in danger. Just this one little thing: Somebody was turning all those bolts. This whole world is just a network of people who work together, serving each other. It's not just because we need to earn a living. That would be putting appreciation back to the level of appraisal. We work because we belong to this great big human family and we want to do our share. And also, of course, we need to earn a living, but that is only one small part of it.

Then you go to a bigger level, the very existence of the world. Why is there something and not just nothing? Only children ask these questions. But there is the child in us who ought to ask these questions. The child in us needs to be cultivated. As somebody said, "Childhood is too short to become the child you are meant to be." An entire life is needed for this child to bloom forth, along with all that is good about this child. Asking this kind of question is really important.

The answer that even our daily language gives to it is: It's a *given* world. We live in a given world—it's a gift—there's no doubt about that. We live in a given place, at a given time. If it is given, the only appropriate answer is gratefulness. Really, what else is there if it's given? Gratefulness.

Most of the time, we can deeply appreciate it without any difficulty—if only we wake up and begin to open our eyes, open our ears, and see what is given to us totally gratis, without us doing anything about it. We ourselves are gifts that we find. When we wake up—when we become conscious, however young we are—we find ourselves as a given. There's very little we can change about it. We can't change the parents we have. We can't change the time when we were born, the country in which we were born, the political situation, the economic situation. We can't change anything about that: We find it as a given.

Now it may not be a given that you fully appreciate, but that's where the next question comes in. If gratefulness is the appreciation of the gratuitously given, what do you when you find yourself in a situation in which you cannot appreciate the circumstances? When you find yourself in a situation of violence, of war, of exploitation, of unfaithfulness in a relationship, of sickness, of untimely death? What do you do in those situations? It is a given—you can't change it, there it is, you must be realistic about it—and you really can't appreciate it fully. What do you do? Well, you have to resort to the one key word that is of extreme importance in the context of gratefulness, and that is *opportunity*. When you look very carefully—even at those moments when you appreciate with great conviction and joy a given situation—what you appreciate is really your ability to enjoy, not the fact that it is there. That's one little thing we need to learn: Whenever we are grateful, we are grateful for an opportunity. Most of the time, this is the opportunity to thoroughly enjoy. You enjoy it only when you become grateful. Before that, you're taking it for granted; you're not enjoying it.

What you're grateful for is the *opportunity* to enjoy. When you keep this in mind, then when you are given something that you cannot appreciate—all those things that are life-denying in the world—this word "opportunity" comes to mind, and you have to ask yourself, "What is this the opportunity for?" You can *always* be grateful for the opportunity, because life always gives you positive gifts, positive opportunities. Even if the surroundings and the circumstances are not to be appreciated, the opportunity is to be appreciated. That is most of the time the opportunity to learn something.

We remember from school—grade school in particular—that there were always all these opportunities to learn given to us. There were always some kids—and the kid in each of us—who didn't want to learn. We had all sorts of other opportunities in mind: playing in the brook, fishing, lying in the sun, climbing around on the rocks, and all sorts of other things that we wanted. But there was nothing we could do: We were sitting in the school, so this was the opportunity given to us.

We find ourselves over and over again with a given that is an opportunity to learn. Even though we didn't enjoy learning very much at that time, it was good for us in retrospect to learn. "In retrospect" is another important aspect of difficult situations in which we find ourselves and ask "Can anybody be grateful for that mess?"

Yes, it is the opportunity to learn something. What is now [being given as] the opportunity to learn? In retrospect, we see that in the past something terribly difficult happened to us that looked like the end of our life—the breakup of everything we treasured, a complete disaster—and now, looking back, we see that it brought new opportunities, brought new ways of living. In retrospect we can see that very clearly. But looking forward, it just looks like a disaster. So we can remind ourselves that just as in the past, a problem led to something helpful, so too in the future it might. I'm not pushing, I'm just suggesting that it *might* lead to something; we cannot persuade ourselves to [be open to] more. But openness for surprise—an openness for something that might happen—is already an opportunity for which we can be grateful.

Those are the important elements of what gratefulness is. It is the appreciation of the gratuitously given opportunity. *Mostly*—I stress that—it is the opportunity to enjoy, but always it is the opportunity to do something with the opportunity given to us, to at least learn something and be creative and expect that there is something helpful coming, and then our openness will show us what this opportunity entails for us.

—*Brother David Steindl-Rast*

A Good Day

You think this is just

another day in your *life?*

It's not just another day;

it's the one day that
is given to you . . .

today.

It's *given* to you. It's a gift.

It's the only gift that you have right now, and the only appropriate response is gratefulness.

If you do nothing else but to
cultivate that response to the great
gift that this unique day is,

if you learn to respond
as if it were the first day
of your life,

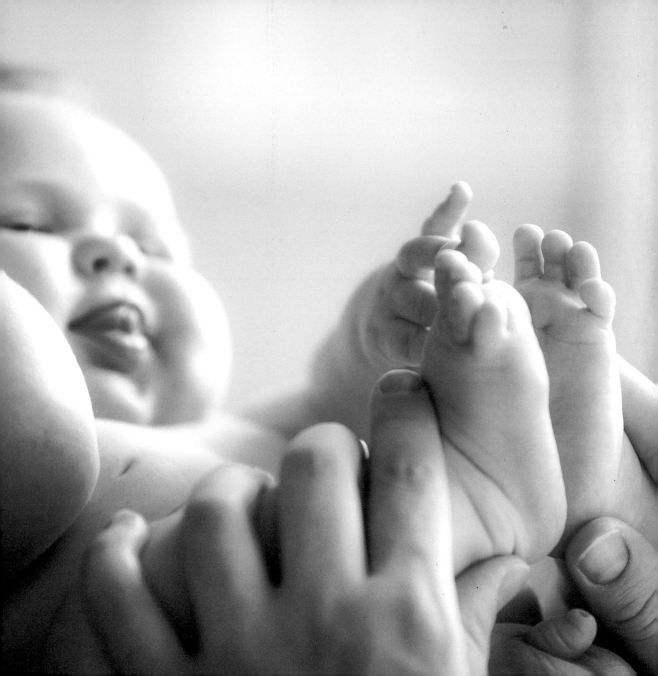

and the very last day,

then you will have spent
this day *very well*.

Begin by *opening* your
eyes and be surprised that you
have eyes you can open,

that incredible array of colors

that is constantly offered to
us for pure enjoyment.

Look at the sky.

We so rarely look at the sky.
We so rarely note how different
it is from *moment to*
moment with clouds coming

and going.

We just think of the weather, and even of the weather we don't think of all the many nuances of weather.

We just think of good weather
and bad weather.

This day right now has unique weather, maybe a kind that will never exactly in that form come again.

The formation of clouds in the sky will never be the same that it is right now.

Open your eyes. Look at that.

Look at the *faces*
of people whom you meet.

Each one has an *incredible*
story behind their face, a story
that you could never fully fathom,

not only their own story,
but the story of their ancestors.
We all go back so far.

And in this *present moment* on this day, all the people you meet, all that life from generations and from so many places all over the world,

flows together and meets you
here like a life-giving
water, if you only open your
heart and drink.

Open your heart
to the incredible gifts that
civilization gives to us.

You flip a switch
and there is
electric light.

You turn a faucet and
there is warm water and cold water—
and drinkable water.
It's a gift that millions and millions
in the world will never experience.

So these are just a few of
an enormous number
of gifts to which you can
open your heart.

And so I wish for you that
you would open your heart
to all these blessings and let
them *flow* through you,

that everyone whom you will meet
on this day will be blessed by *you*;
just by your eyes,

by your smile, by your touch—
just by your presence.

Let the gratefulness overflow
into blessing all around you,

and then it will really be

Afterword

*"If the only prayer you ever say in your entire life is
'thank you,' it would be enough."*

—Meister Eckhart

I was raised on gratitude. My parents were Holocaust survivors who came to this country with nothing more than the clothes on their backs. They met after the war, came to America, moved to Brooklyn, had a family, and made a wonderful life. As teenagers during the Holocaust, my parents didn't experience nature in their upbringing. As a child growing up in New York, neither did I. My closest nature experience was racing Popsicle sticks down a gutter in Brooklyn. Living under their roof, I saw how they were grateful for every blessing that came their way: sunshine, the most humble of foods, a roof over their heads, a job—and most importantly, having children. To them, that was heaven on earth. Their thankful attitude had a profound affect on me. Through their eyes, I learned that even the smallest of things—a wildflower growing out of a crack in the sidewalk, and the ordinary things—another sunny morning, were just as important and just as deserving of attention as the once-in-a-while, extraordinary things. They are all worthy of celebrating through the lens of gratitude.

While at UCLA, I fell in love with photography and filmmaking. I discovered my voice. Filming Nature is when I met my greatest teacher. She taught me the art of composition, lighting, movement, and beauty. More importantly, she led me down a path of self-discovery, making me curious to explore new horizons, to reveal the universal patterns and rhythms that are a part of my soul, looking into a mirror to discover truth and beauty.

Nature has taught me how to live a creative and sustainable life. Beauty and seduction are nature's tools for survival because we protect what we fall in love with. You can detail all the shocking facts about environmental degradation, but unless you move people emotionally there won't be the shift in consciousness we need to solve our problems. Intellectually we have all the answers needed to affect change; what we lack is the will. What could be more important than sustaining life on the planet, having respect and awe for all living creatures? Since everything in the world wears out, nature invented reproduction as a mechanism for DNA to stream forward, as a life force that passes right through us and makes us a link in the evolution of life. We do stand on the shoulders of our ancestors. There are values to be learned by observing nature. She does not waste a single molecule, and never takes more than what she needs. It is all about efficiency and symbiotic relationships. So aren't we grateful for our eyes that can convert light energy to an electrical impulse that is sent to our brains in order to explore our world? Aren't we grateful that we have hearts that can feel these vibrations, to experience the pleasure and beauty of nature? Nature's beauty is a gift that cultivates appreciation and gratitude, filling us with wonder and wisdom while opening our hearts.

I never get tired of capturing the rhythms of life that are beyond our perception. We see life at 24 frames per second, a narrow point of view. I have been continuously filming time-lapse flowers for 24 hours a day, 7 days a week, for over 35 years, capturing 2 seconds of screen time per day totaling 12 hours of content—so I have compressed 30 years into 12 hours. Today with digital high-tech cameras I can film at 1,000 frames per second and capture 12 hours of slow-motion imagery in one hour. What is truly amazing is that when played back, the graceful, poetic, symphonic motion of the time-lapse flower or the slow-motion hummingbird is the same, yet they come from two opposite ends of the time spectrum. Humans look like time-lapse ants to a redwood tree and we look like a slow-motion giant to a mosquito. My heart still jumps for joy watching the flowers come alive, dancing to the light, a process I will never get tired of.

I have an inquisitive mind that wants to unveil the mysteries of the world; from social behavior to cultural history, it is all fascinating to me. The patterns and systems you see in civilization mirror the ecosystems that you see in nature. We are a part of nature, not apart from it, so this should come as no surprise. So I use time lapse as way of preserving a time capsule of natural history.

My film library of magic moments is my visual vocabulary. As I travel the world, I try to film magic moments. I capture concepts and images that are like words. My library of magic moments is my visual vocabulary. For me, putting *Gratitude* together is like creating a poem—illustrating different feelings and emotions that relate to gratitude. At times, these prized moments can be just a look in someone's eye or the touch between two people, or the diversity of people doing the same thing, whether

you're Christian, Jew, Muslim, Hindu, or Buddhist. We all raise our kids the best we can. We all try to make a living, to have food, and shelter. It's the same story all over the world. In my library there are images of people from different regions with different languages, food, clothing, and economic scales. The images convey how we're all connected. I gravitate to stories about people who have overcome adversity and have developed a positive attitude, which indicates they've developed a grateful heart.

But life has challenges and sometimes makes people close their hearts. A bad experience can harden the heart. There's no limit to how big your heart can be, or how many people you can love. Gratitude is a great exercise. It's a heart opener. It's an exercise we need, one we long for. We need heart openers.

Clearly people are hungry to give thanks. In a time when so many have so little, people are waking up to how good it feels to appreciate what they do have. Self-help books on gratitude are routinely best-sellers. Quotes on gratitude are among the most shared on Facebook and Twitter.

Back in early 2000, while working on my film *America's Heart and Soul* for Disney, I had the gift of traveling across the country to capture stories of remarkable yet ordinary people who shared with me their wisdom and passion for living. After completing the film, I realized that because of my parents' Holocaust experience I was attracted to these real-life stories of people who had overcome adversity yet still had joy in their lives. I then began to wonder why some people had the ability to overcome these obstacles, while others fell victim to suffering and despair. That is when I began developing my next project, *Gratitude Revealed*. I met composer Gary Malkin, whose *Graceful Passages* CD inspired me with his gift of combining transformational music and spoken words. He offered me the opportunity to visually illustrate some of his recordings, and when I heard Brother David's "A Good Day," I was moved to tears. The depth of wisdom in Brother David's words and the empathy in his voice, combined with Gary's elegant music, touched the deepest part of my soul. So as a "proof of concept" I edited my visual to the soundtrack and I presented it at the end of my TEDxSF presentation on beauty and nature. TEDxSF posted it on YouTube and it went viral, sending ripples out to over four million viewers to date.

The amount of mail and comments from viewers who have watched the *Gratitude* video is astonishing; powerful, moving letters from individuals who are in the throes of incurable illness, survivors of emotional trauma, parents who have lost a child and who have now found a way to cope by being grateful for the time they shared with them. Some use it as a video alarm clock, to watch every morning to align themselves as they face a new day. Teenagers, mothers, fathers, grandmothers, grandfathers, people from all around the globe and from all walks of life, write to tell me how their own gratitude has made their lives possible—and how *Gratitude* has deeply touched, inspired, and changed their lives.

It is with an immensely grateful heart that I share with you some of the comments I have received. These are the ripples that have rebounded off people's hearts and found their way back to us:

"This is a video that should automatically turn on every morning as you awake, replacing your alarm clock with gentle music and a wonderful message to carry with you throughout each day."

"I am healing from cardiac surgery and each day I wake is a gift of life and viewing this incredible video I found myself in a pool of tears . . . tears of happiness . . . thank you for enhancing my life with this surprising gift."

"I will watch this video every morning every day for the rest of my life."

"We are bombarded with so much electronic media everyday, but sometimes something really beautiful grabs your attention and cuts through all the noise and makes you stand still and think about what it means to have gratitude. This video is like an early morning stroll in a forest."

"I really love watching this video over and over again. It opens our eyes to every wonderful thing around us that sometimes we forgot to be grateful of. Being grateful everyday is like making everyday a good day. :)"

"Inspiring, beautiful, poignant, and moving. Tears flowed as gratitude rose from the depths of my being. As a cancer survivor and a person who has health challenges, I am so blessed for every day as I remember to be consciously aware of every moment, every breath and every gift. Thank you for this gift! ;-)"

"I can't stop watching this. It reaches into me and grabs my inner soul in a way I haven't experienced in a long time. Thank you to its creators for giving this gift to us!

"THIS HAS TO BE THE MOST BREATHTAKING AND INSPIRING VIDEO ON ALL OF YOUTUBE! IT NEEDS A BILLION VIEWS!"

"Thank you. This should be compulsory viewing in every school and for every politician."

"I sat and watched your film several times before I forwarded it to many friends out in the world. As I watched the beauty you captured in your images, I realized I had been unaware of tears flowing down my face. Not tears of sadness, but I was moved to feel great compassion for the interconnected beauty all around us. I work with children who have been damaged by life, to whom circumstances or environment has been unkind. I will show your film to them... and maybe, just maybe, it's gentle unfolding can open them, if even for a brief moment, to the beautiful wonder of the world. Thank you."

"This is my church and the way I want to live my life. Thank you so much."

"I shared your video Gratitude with Lisa, who lost her beloved daughter, Tammy, a few years ago to an aggressive form of cancer. Lisa wrote and said after viewing your video, she no longer just 'goes on each day' or dwells on her loss. Each day, she remembers the 'fantastically' good times she shared with Tammy and cherishes the memories. Thank you."

A montage from my theatrical feature the *Beauty of Pollination* received 22.6 million views worldwide, averaging 100,000 each day. The fact that so many people have responded to my films, which basically present the wonder and awe of nature, is proof that there is a hunger out there that needs nourishment. I'm just a conduit for that experience. Experiencing the grandeur of nature makes you feel humble, reverent, and inspired. Those are great things that open your heart.

When people see my images, a lot of times they will say, "Oh my God." Have you ever wondered what that means? The "oh" means it caught your attention—it makes you present, it makes you mindful. The "my" means it connects with something deep inside your soul, it creates a gateway for your inner voice to rise up and be heard. And God, "God" is that personal journey we all want to be on, to be inspired, to feel like we are connected to a universe that celebrates life.

I've captured nature so that people can experience this kind of heart opener if, for whatever reason, they can't be in nature. Obviously we're all busy. There are so many kids who grow up underprivileged, who never get an opportunity to go out in nature or ever see the ocean. I am grateful that through my images and my films, I can remind people that every day is a gift.

Since most people don't live in rural areas, we are disconnected from nature. So if we can experience truth and beauty through the digital distribution of nature and art, than I hope we can reawaken people's spirits and facilitate the consciousness shift that must happen in order to create a sustainable future. The joy for me, as a filmmaker, is making these visual images of nature accessible to everyone. I've always felt that the combination of music and visuals can shift people's consciousness, to inspire them.

That's what art should do. It has led to the inception of Moving Art™ (movingart.tv), a channel I am developing for multiple platforms that will allow you to fill your home with nature, cityscapes, and inspirational montages. It is my hope that this collection of groundbreaking 2D and 3D images will get people to fall in love with nature and our world so that we will take better care of it.

To be grateful is to be mindful. Nature's beauty opens our hearts to feel wonder and compassion. Our gratitude will help us get back on the path to ensure the earth is a beautiful, healthy, sustainable home for the plants and animals, for me and you, for our children, our grandchildren, and beyond.

—*Louie Schwartzberg*

From the Creator of the Audio Montage of Brother David's Spoken Message and Music

There's something about the way our voices sound when we're fully embodying them. Each of our voices is unique, like hieroglyphic thumbprints of who we *truly* are. Some people embody their essence so fully, the very sound of their voices can mysteriously soothe us, conveying an experience of what feels nourishing and true, the way it felt when, as children, we were being "tucked in" by our parents as a story was being read to us before we gently fell asleep.

That's how it felt when I listened to Brother David Steindl-Rast that autumn day as I was recording him for a project his nonprofit commissioned me (and a friend) to produce. We had been asked to create a recording that would make it possible for people to hear direct testimonies from those who believed in the mission and vision of Brother David's nonprofit, A Network for Grateful Living, as part of a new funding campaign. Little did I know that this simple message Brother David shared with me that day—for which I ultimately composed the music—would be shared with literally *millions* of people from all over the world, thanks to the inspiring artistry of award-winning filmmaker, Louis Schwartzberg.

I have been recording heart-opening messages from those whom we call "wisdom keepers" for many years now. No matter how famous these people were, my creative partner and I would invite them to share an extemporaneous message directly from their heart to humanity, as if humanity were one, solitary person. However, the real magic inside these messages was revealed when we added original music.

Most of us know that music has the power to arouse our emotions like few other art forms can do. When we enhanced these messages with music, we learned that these spoken word and music montages made it possible for the listener to hear these messages not only with their ears—*but with their hearts as well*. As a result, we felt that if enough of these messages could be disseminated, we would be playing *our* part towards spreading greater compassion, forgiveness, loving kindness—and gratitude—during these remarkable times of challenge and change.

Created by a true artist with a lifetime commitment to the transformative power of visual beauty, Louis Schwartzberg's *Gratitude* offers us a visual piece of transcendence, resulting in a form of media artistry that is shamanic in its power, accessible to anyone from any cultural or socio-economic background, disarmingly simple and perfect in execution. This piece also demonstrates what happens when we can collaboratively bring a diversity of talents together—creating a whole so much greater than the sum of the parts.

By honoring who many consider to be "the Godfather of the Gratitude Movement" in this way, Brother David's lifetime message has been immortalized and preserved for future generations to experience again and again, ensuring that the universal value of gratitude will forever be enshrined as a core value to the human experience. Thank you, Louie and Brother David, for giving me the honor of participating in an unexpected and thrilling artistic adventure that will hopefully be the first of many of these soulful expressions of wisdom, music, and images to be created in the future.

—*Gary Malkin*